Content-Based Langu

This module explores the content-driven approach to language teaching, or the teaching of nonlinguistic content such as geography, history, or science using the target language. It lays out effective techniques that help facilitate students' comprehension of curricular content and also discusses how teacher collaboration and students' L1s affect this approach to language teaching. With an instructional sequence comprising noticing, awareness, and practice activities as well as examples of content-and-language integrated units, the *Content-Based Language Teaching* module is the ideal main textbook for instructors seeking a clear and practical treatment of the topic for their courses, which can also be taught in conjunction with other modules in the series.

Roy Lyster is Professor of Second Language Education in the Department of Integrated Studies Education at McGill University, Canada.

The Routledge E-Modules on Contemporary Language Teaching
Series Editors: Bill VanPatten, Michigan State University, USA, and Gregory D. Keating, San Diego State University, USA

For a full list of titles in this series, please visit www.routledge.com

The *Routledge E-Modules on Contemporary Language Teaching* series is an exciting and innovative approach to topics for the novice or in-training teacher of languages. Written in an easily accessible style and delivered in e-format and paperback versions, specialists and experts provide the latest thinking on a variety of issues that form the foundation of language-teacher knowledge and practice: the nature of language and communication, second-language acquisition, interactive tasks, assessment, focus on form, vocabulary development, and technology in language teaching, among many others. Each module serves as a self-contained unit to be used on its own or as part of an introductory course on language teaching. Instructors may "mix and match" modules to create their own readings for a course on language teaching. The modules may serve as primary reading or as supplemental reading, with each module offering points of reflection, discussion questions, self-quizzes, and a reading list for those who wish to delve further into the topic.

Vocabulary in Language Teaching
By Joe Barcroft

Interactive Tasks
By Michael J. Leeser and Justin P. White

Focusing on Form in Language Instruction
By Wynne Wong and Daphnée Simard

Technology in Language Learning: An Overview
By Bryan Smith

Teaching Second Language Writing
By Charlene Polio

Content-Based Language Teaching
By Roy Lyster

Content-Based Language Teaching

Roy Lyster

Routledge
Taylor & Francis Group

NEW YORK AND LONDON

First published 2018
by Routledge
711 Third Avenue, New York, NY 10017

and by Routledge
2 Park Square, Milton Park, Abingdon, Oxon, OX14 4RN

Routledge is an imprint of the Taylor & Francis Group, an informa business

© 2018 Taylor & Francis

Every effort has been made to contact copyright-holders. Please advise the
publisher of any errors or omissions, and these will be corrected in
subsequent editions.

Library of Congress Cataloging-in-Publication Data
A catalog record for this title has been requested

ISBN: 978-1-138-10306-1 (pbk)
ISBN: 978-1-315-10303-7 (ebk)

Typeset in Sabon
by Apex CoVantage, LLC

Visit the companion website to preview and purchase other modules in
this series: http://routledgetextbooks.com/textbooks/9781315679594/

Content-Based Language Teaching

Roy Lyster

Overview

This module will guide you to explore the following topics:

- The wide range of program types and contexts that compose CBLT
- The benefits and challenges of learning language through content
- Scaffolding techniques that make content comprehensible for L2 learners
- Effective questioning and feedback techniques for CBLT
- An instructional sequence comprising noticing, awareness, and practice activities
- Examples of content-and-language integrated units
- The role of teacher collaboration in CBLT
- The role of the students' L1 in CBLT

Contexts of CBLT

Content-based language teaching (CBLT) is an instructional approach in which nonlinguistic content such as geography, history, or science is taught to students through the medium of a language that they are learning as an additional language. A major focus of CBLT is the development of literacy and academic ability with language. CBLT is a more effective and motivating way to develop such abilities than more traditional grammar-based approaches. Whereas traditional methods isolate the target language from content other than the language itself, CBLT enriches classroom discourse through substantive content in a way that provides both a cognitive basis for language learning and a motivational basis for purposeful communication. Based on the premise that the best way to learn a second or foreign language (L2) is by using it rather than studying about it, CBLT provides learners with many opportunities for meaningful and purposeful language use. CBLT, however, does not preclude language instruction. Instead, CBLT promotes its integration through a counter-balanced approach that entails a dynamic interplay between language and content.

CBLT comes in many different shapes and sizes and in fact is called by other names and acronyms, including **content-based instruction** (CBI) and **content and language integrated learning** (CLIL). Whether called CBLT, CBI, or CLIL, a range of instructional initiatives can be identified along a continuum with **language-driven** programs at one end and **content-driven** programs at the other end (see Figure 1).

At the language-driven end of the spectrum are some foreign-language classes that promote target-language development by incorporating a focus on themes or topics with which learners have some familiarity in their L1 (e.g., seasons and weather, sports and hobbies, travel and vacations) as a means of developing target-language vocabulary. Such themes provide opportunities for language practice but without high-stakes assessment of students' content knowledge, such as tests that need to be passed in order to move to a higher level, to get a job, or to be admitted as a student to a particular institution. Still other foreign language classes may integrate more challenging themes (e.g., environmental issues, bullying, discrimination) not only to enrich classroom discourse but also to make connections to the "real world" while developing students' advanced thinking and literacy skills. Students who have been primed by their instructional setting to be form oriented benefit from theme-based tasks designed to orient their attention toward meaning and to avert an overemphasis on form, which may otherwise jeopardize the development of their communicative abilities.

Toward the middle of the continuum are program models in which students study one or two subjects in the target language, usually in tandem with a foreign language or language arts class. This is the model adopted by many CLIL programs in Europe and elsewhere. There are many varieties of CLIL, but its prototypical implementation involves at least one or more content classes taught in a foreign language, which in most cases is English, in addition to a class in English as a foreign language. The acronym CLIL can also be used as a generic umbrella term for bilingual

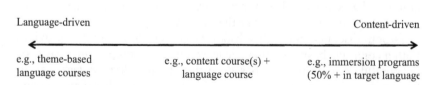

Language-driven   Content-driven

e.g., theme-based   e.g., content course(s) +   e.g., immersion programs
language courses   language course   (50% + in target language

Figure 1 Range of CBLT Settings

content-based education in the same way that CBLT is being used in this module.

Also in the middle of the continuum is the English-medium CBLT program implemented in China that teaches content areas that are not part of the formal curriculum such as "nature and society" and "science and life," usually for two lessons per week at the middle-school level. At the University of Ottawa in Canada an adjunct model of CBLT has been adopted that enables nonfrancophone students to take regular content courses offered in French with francophone students for whom the content courses were originally designed. At the same time, the nonfrancophone students are sheltered as a group in a separate adjunct language course that focuses on understanding the content of the course. Also at the postsecondary level, language and literature departments often offer upper-level undergraduate content courses in the target language, such as social and physical geography courses or courses structured around cultural or literary themes.

At the content-driven end of the spectrum are school-based **one-way immersion** programs. One-way immersion programs provide a substantial portion of students' subject-matter instruction through the medium of a language that they are learning as a second, foreign, heritage, or indigenous language. The remaining proportion of the curriculum is provided through the medium of a shared primary language, which normally has majority status in the community. At the elementary level, at least 50% of the curriculum is taught through the immersion language, whereas continuation programs at the secondary level include a minimum of two subject courses in the immersion language. Because a defining characteristic of immersion is its aim for additive bilingualism (i.e., learning an additional language with no threat of losing the first language), programs that do not maintain parallel instruction in at least two languages (such as the so-called structured English immersion programs in the United States) are not considered to be real immersion programs.

Immersion programs have been adopted in some countries to promote the learning of a second co-official language. Examples of these include French immersion in Canada, Swedish immersion in Finland, Catalan immersion in Spain, Basque immersion in Spain, and Irish immersion in Ireland. In still other contexts, school-based CBLT programs have been designed to deliver at least half the curriculum through the medium of a regional language such as Breton and Occitan in France or an indigenous language such as Maori in New Zealand, Hawaiian in the state of Hawaii, and Cherokee in the state of Oklahoma. English as an international language is the target language of a variety of CBLT programs ranging from early immersion in Japan and Brazil to late immersion in Hong Kong.

Two-way immersion programs normally integrate a similar number of children from two different mother-tongue backgrounds. In the United

States, for example, there are many Spanish/English two-way immersion programs that provide curricular instruction in both Spanish and English to classes consisting of some students whose L1 is Spanish and others whose L1 is English. Most two-way immersion programs follow either a 50/50 model or a 90/10 model, with the greater proportion of time allocated to the minority language. In contrast, students in one-way immersion programs normally share a common primary language and are all learning the immersion language as an additional language.

Often thought of as an extension of CLIL programs, English as a medium of instruction (**EMI**) in higher education is a rapidly expanding area of content-based instruction in many countries where English is not an official language. That is, universities are increasingly offering programs in English rather than in the national language in order to facilitate mobility and to attract more international students. This is sometimes referred to as "integrating content and language in higher education," but most research in these contexts has confirmed that little emphasis is placed on developing proficiency in English. EMI has grown exponentially in Europe as a result of the Erasmus Program (also known as the European Region Action Scheme for the Mobility of University Students). Since its inception, the Erasmus Program has enabled almost 3 million students to complete a part of their studies abroad. This program enables not only Erasmus participants but also local students to study content through a language other than their L1.

Yet another context for CBLT at the content-driven end of the continuum includes schools where minority-language students find themselves without any L1 support in mainstream classrooms; this is sometimes referred to as **submersion**. Often the children of immigrants, these students may be left to their own devices to deal with the switch from a home language to the school language. In many U.S. schools, however, **content-based ESL** and **sheltered instruction** programs are available to better address the needs of minority-language students who are learning English while also learning curricular content through English. In content-based ESL, teachers incorporate information from content areas as a means to improve students' English-language proficiency. Sheltered instruction entails content courses for ESL learners taught normally by content (rather than ESL) specialists. These contexts have given rise to a useful teacher development tool known as the Sheltered Instruction Observation Protocol (SIOP), which provides teachers with guidance in teaching subject-matter content in English to students whose L1 is not English. It includes techniques that make the content material accessible while maintaining grade-level objectives and developing literacy skills as well as skills specific to L2 learners.

CBLT thus crosses a wide range of international contexts and instructional settings, including elementary, secondary, and postsecondary institutions. In spite of the tremendous differences across these contexts (some including majority-language and others minority-language students), there are some common pedagogical issues that arise at the interface of language and content teaching. These concerns are addressed next.

Convergent Concerns in CBLT

Research has consistently shown that the outcomes of CBLT are positive when the conditions for its implementation are favorable. Favorable conditions include the availability of teacher training and support, instructional resources, and threshold levels of proficiency on the part of both teachers and students. A common finding across such contexts is that students demonstrate high levels of motivation and satisfaction while improving their comprehension skills and attaining higher levels of communicative ability than students in more traditional instructional settings focused solely on language.

Research has also shown that students' target-language accuracy tends to be less developed than their overall communicative abilities. For example, immersion students are known to develop high levels of communicative ability but lower-than-expected levels of grammatical accuracy, lexical variety, and sociolinguistic appropriateness. It has become clear in CBLT that many target-language features, especially (but not limited to) those involving morphosyntax, are not learned "by osmosis" and instead require a more intentional instructional focus.

These findings led to the assertion that content teaching on its own is not necessarily good language teaching and needs to be manipulated and complemented in ways that maximize target-language learning. Otherwise, use of the target language to teach content has limitations in terms of the range of language forms and functions to which it exposes students. A good example of this is the distribution of verb tenses used by French immersion teachers: 74–75% in the present tense or imperative forms, 14–15% in the past tense, and 3% in the conditional. In a study described by Merrill Swain, a Canadian immersion teacher was observed using the immediate future tense to teach a history lesson about events that took place more than 200 years ago. While such a strategy might bring the historical events much closer to students, it does nothing to help them understand the meaning of various past-tense forms in French and goes a long way toward explaining their inaccurate use of these forms. Moreover, most school-level history textbooks in French are now written in the present tense, thus limiting students' exposure to meaningful instances of past-tense forms in the written input as well.

Another concern about content teaching on its own is that it can take on a lecture format without providing sufficient opportunities for interaction and student production. A driving force underlying CBLT has been the central role of input in acquisition, whereby acquisition occurs as learners engage in actively comprehending meaning in the nonprimary language (see the module on acquisition by Gregory D. Keating in the Routledge Series). What is more, scholars such as Stephen Krashen have claimed that for input to be beneficial for acquisition, it must be comprehensible. Thus, underlying CBLT is the idea that content learning happens via **comprehensible input**. Early observations of CBLT revealed that instructors had a tendency to make their classes primarily input driven, striving to make the content comprehensible and drawing attention especially to vocabulary, while leaving students with limited opportunities to produce the language.

Instructional techniques that ensure the comprehension of subject matter taught through the medium of the students' L2 are at the core of CBLT and are essential for students' academic success. The notion that learners can and should be exposed to language just ahead of their current level of ability, rather than being exposed only to language they already know, is essential to CBLT. At the same time, however, empirical research has revealed that the quantity and quality of the input to which CBLT exposes students may be insufficient to ensure continued L2 growth (see the earlier discussion about the lack of past tense in teaching history). For learners aspiring to reach beyond beginner-levels of proficiency and to develop literacy skills in the target language, an exclusively input-driven approach to language instruction may not help them achieve these aspirations because students may rely on comprehension strategies that bypass a reliance on structure to get meaning. They may rely more on vocabulary, real-world knowledge, and inference to comprehend language sufficiently without processing structural elements in the language. Bypassing language structure in this way, however, is harder to do when producing the language. For this reason, producing the target language in contexts of interaction is considered to be a key part of the learning process in CBLT. Having to produce the target language allows students to become more aware of language structure—if they are pushed to convey their meaning in precise and comprehensible ways. This is called **pushed output**.

There is now considerable interest in identifying instructional practices in CBLT that will enable students to attain high levels of target-language proficiency, not only for the sake of greater accuracy but also for enhancing their ability to engage with the type of complex language that is key to academic literacy and school success. The remainder of this module addresses various instructional practices that promote continued L2 development while enabling students to engage with subject matter taught through the L2.

Teacher Scaffolding

At the core of CBLT is teacher **scaffolding**. Scaffolding refers to the assistance that a teacher provides to students so that they can understand language and accomplish tasks in ways that they would be unable to do on their own without such support. Thus, while one type of scaffolding assists students in understanding content presented through their L2, another type supports them in productively using the L2 to engage with the content. Such scaffolding is essential to successful CBLT.

Teachers have at their disposal a wide range of scaffolding strategies that facilitate students' comprehension of curricular content taught through the target language. For example, teachers can build redundancy into their speech to convey similar meanings in various ways by using self-repetition and paraphrase, as well as multiple examples, definitions, and synonyms. In tandem with their verbal input, teachers can use props, graphs, and other graphic organizers, as well as visual and multimedia resources. To further facilitate comprehension, teachers can rely on body language, including gestures, facial expressions, and a range of other such paralinguistic elements. This type of teacher scaffolding helps to answer the burning question of how students can understand increasingly complex subject matter presented through their L2. Students can draw on the contextual clues provided in the scaffolding, while also drawing on their own prior knowledge about the topic, in order to engage with content in a language they know only partially.

Scaffolding the interaction to facilitate comprehension, however, needs to be seen as a temporary support, similar to the role of scaffolding in the construction industry. That is, students need to develop increasingly more advanced comprehension strategies that enable them to process the target language autonomously without the scaffolding. Instructional techniques that rely too much on linguistic redundancy, gestures, and other visual and nonlinguistic support are unlikely over time to make the kinds of increasing demands on the learners' language system that are necessary for continued L2 learning. This means that teachers need to engage in a delicate balancing act of providing, on one hand, just the right amount of support to make the target language comprehensible, while being demanding enough, on the other hand, to ensure that learners engage in higher-order cognitive skills. In other words, teachers need to avoid simplifying the curricular content and, instead, need to challenge students to interact with increasingly complex academic content. Teachers have been observed doing so by structuring their lessons as cyclical rather than linear to ensure an exploration of the content from multiple perspectives instead of as a list of facts. Teachers need to draw on students' prior knowledge while helping them to engage in deeper levels of processing. In this way, students develop technical academic knowledge and move beyond the realm of only common-sense everyday knowledge.

Teachers need also to provide support for their students to use the target language productively. First, in their own interaction with students, teachers need to give students appropriate wait time to interpret questions and formulate responses. Second, they need to create many opportunities for students to use the target language, including role plays, debates, and presentations, while also using a variety of interactive groupings in order to promote learning from and with peers (e.g., peer editing, peer tutoring, peer correction). Oral interaction between teacher and students as well as among peers is considered an important catalyst for L2 development in CBLT.

Reflection

Read these very different teacher profiles of two 7th-grade science classes in French immersion published by Day and Shapson (see Readings at the end of the module). Which of these sounds more like someone focused on content and communicative development at the same time?

Claudette's science class

Claudette's language-rich science classroom is a veritable arena of communication. Her students engage in both "doing" science and collaboratively talking about it, as she gives them increasing responsibility for their learning. Claudette encourages students to speculate, justify, and be comfortable with the view that there might be "no right answer" to some questions, even though she has specific learning objectives and structures her classes accordingly. There are many opportunities for students to produce the immersion language and to communicate with one another about what is being learned, enabling them to use a variety of language forms and functions.

Michel's science class

Michel often begins lessons by drawing on his students' knowledge to introduce the textbook material, but he does not encourage much discussion or exploration of their answers, expecting instead that their responses conform to predetermined categories. Michel repeats or rephrases what they say, writes their answers on the board, and asks them to take notes. He speaks clearly, provides a good model of the immersion language, but elaborates very little. Students rarely give more than one-word or one-phrase answers, and there is little interaction among them. Language is used for communication mainly between the teacher and the students.

A Counterbalanced Approach to CBLT

As alluded to earlier, there is a growing consensus in the research literature that, for CBLT to reach its full potential for developing high levels of target-language proficiency, it needs to integrate a more intentional focus on language rather than focusing only on content. While researchers concur that the language focus in CBLT needs to be less incidental and more intentional, they do not appeal to sudden injections of traditional language instruction that focus on form alone at the expense of content (e.g., drills). Instead, recommendations for increasing the effectiveness of CBLT promote a more seamless integration of a focus on language in the context of subject-matter instruction.

One way for teachers to integrate language and content in CBLT is by emphasizing the ways in which linguistic features of discipline-specific language construe particular kinds of meanings. This involves making students explicitly aware of (a) the academic language functions they need to understand and communicate in specific academic disciplines (e.g., describing, comparing, explaining, hypothesizing, predicting) and (b) the conventional text structures or genres that are characteristic of particular disciplines (e.g., science reports, historical accounts, math problems, essays).

Another way for teachers to integrate language and content is to intentionally draw attention to language in discourse contexts related to subject matter or literacy themes in ways that support students' subsequent use of the target features in interactive situations. This involves giving content and language objectives complementary status and shifting students' attention between language and content through a counterbalanced approach to CBLT. The shift is toward language if the classroom is primarily content driven and toward content if the overall classroom context is predominantly language driven.

The purpose of shifting students' attention between content and language is to strengthen their metalinguistic awareness and to foster depth of processing. Metalinguistic awareness is what students need to detect patterns in the input, whereas depth of processing refers to the extent to which a learner reflects on new information and links it to previous knowledge. The greater the depth of processing, the greater the likelihood that information will be stored in long-term memory and become more readily accessible. Processing disciplinary content while also attending to the language that encodes the content is one way for students to engage with increasingly complex language, which is key to academic literacy and success in school-based CBLT.

A counterbalanced approach to CBLT is either reactive or proactive, but, for optimal effectiveness, both are best implemented in tandem. A **reactive approach** includes scaffolding techniques such as questions and feedback in response to students' language production that serve to support student participation while ensuring that oral interaction is a key source of learning. A **proactive approach** includes preplanned activities with intertwined content and language objectives that aim to engage students with language features that might otherwise not be used or even noticed in classrooms focusing on content. These approaches are discussed in more detail next.

Reactive Counterbalanced Instruction

Reactive approaches allow teachers to integrate content and language in seemingly spontaneous ways. Ostensibly unplanned opportunities can take the form of (a) teacher questions intended to increase both the quantity and quality of student output and (b) a range of corrective feedback types, including recasts, prompts, and explicit correction (to be discussed later). Questioning and feedback techniques together provide learners with the scaffolding they need in order to understand, participate, and engage with both language and content.

Teacher Questions

Research on classroom discourse has identified the **IRF sequence** as the most typical teaching exchange: an initiating (I) move by the teacher; a responding (R) move by the student; and a feedback (F) move by the teacher. The IRF sequence is the standard of transmission models of teaching and typical of teacher-centered classrooms. It has been criticized for engaging students only minimally and for maintaining unequal power relationships between teachers and students. Nevertheless, the IRF sequence continues to permeate classroom discourse, probably because it helps teachers to monitor students' knowledge and understanding. By assessing their students in an ongoing manner in the course of interaction, teachers are better equipped to plan and evaluate CBLT.

IRF exchanges can develop into more equal dialogue if, in the third turn, the teacher avoids evaluation and instead requests justifications or counterarguments. This is important because even the simplest of teachers' comments such as "very good" have been shown to inhibit learning opportunities. They inhibit learning by serving a "finale" function that precludes further attempts by others to articulate their understanding or explore alternative answers. In this regard, the feedback move should not be restricted to an evaluative function but rather should serve as a follow-up move that aims to:

a.   Elaborate on the student's response or provide clarification.
b.   Request further elaboration, justification, explanation, or exemplification.
c.   Challenge students' views.

This kind of push helps students to deepen their understanding of ideas and concepts and provides opportunities for students to use language that is more complex than that found in the shorter answers that are more typical of CBLT discourse. This kind of questioning is often called dialogic teaching, which fits well with best practices in CBLT for integrating content and language through purposeful interaction. Dialogic teaching guides learning by drawing on students' curiosity while promoting the co-construction of meaning and the development of critical thinking skills.

Reflection

When asking good questions, teachers need to use a variety of comprehension questions that go beyond the ubiquitous *yes/no* question "Do you all understand?" Students tend to all nod their heads affirmatively in response to such questions. Instead, teachers should ask questions that elicit answers from students that actually demonstrate their comprehension. What might these questions look like?

Corrective Feedback

The way in which teachers interact with their students is central to CBLT. In particular, corrective feedback (CF) provided during teacher-student interaction is one way for teachers to integrate a focus on language into their instructional practices. In contexts of CBLT, CF generally includes recasts, explicit correction, and prompts.

A *recast* is the teacher's reformulation of all or part of a student's utterance, minus anything nonnative-like (in this particular case, the student used the wrong verb to express someone being cold):

S: *Parce qu'elle est trop froid pour aller dans toutes les . . .* [Because she is too cold to go into all the . . .]
T: *Parce qu'elle a trop froid, OK.* [Because she is too cold, OK.]

Explicit correction also provides the correct form but, unlike recasts, clearly indicates that what the student had said was incorrect:

S: *Nous coupons les pailles en six différents grosseurs et attache les pailles avec le ruban gommé.* [We cut the straws into six different thicknesses and attach the straws with tape.]
T: *Euh, David, excuse-moi. Je veux que tu te serves du mot "longueur." Vous avez coupé les pailles en différentes longueurs. Pas grosseurs.* [Uh, David, excuse me. I want you to use the word "length." You cut the straws into different lengths. Not thicknesses.]

Prompts withhold correct forms and instead provide clues to prompt students to retrieve these forms from their current knowledge. There are four types:

1. *Elicitations* enable teachers to elicit self-repair either by asking *wh*-questions or by pausing to allow students to complete the teacher's utterance:

   S: *Once upon a time, there lives a poor girl named Cinderella.*
   T: *Once upon a time, there . . .?*

2. *Clarification requests* include utterances such as "Pardon?" and "I don't understand" that teachers use in response to learner errors to elicit self-correction and often to feign incomprehension:

   S: *When they fire the books.*
   T: *What do you mean "when they fire the books"?*

3. *Repetitions* reproduce the error verbatim, often with rising intonation to highlight the error:

   S: *Il bond.* [It jump.]
   T: *Il bond?* [It jump?]

4. *Metalinguistic clues* include comments, information, or questions about the form of the student's utterance; the following example is triggered by the student's use of a masculine (M) rather than a feminine (F) possessive determiner:

   S: *Parce qu'elle cherche, euh, son carte.* [Because she's looking for, um, her (M) card.]
   T: *Pas son carte.* [Not her (M) card.]

Findings from observational studies conducted in a range of CBLT settings indicate that teachers use recasts, prompts, and explicit correction in similar proportions, with recasts being by far the most frequent, followed by prompts and then explicit correction. Recasts are thus frequent in CBLT but are not necessarily used by teachers to draw students' attention to nonnative-like performance. Instead, recasts can be used to maintain the flow of subject-matter instruction while providing helpful scaffolding to learners when target forms are beyond their abilities. For this reason, recasts can easily be perceived by young learners as confirmations of the content or veracity of their utterances. This occurs because teachers frequently repeat students' well-formed utterances in order to confirm referential meaning and often to "rebroadcast" the student's message to ensure that the whole class has heard. As for the students, they are left to their own devices to figure out whether the teacher's response was mere repetition/confirmation or a recast of a nonnative-like utterance.

Given the potential confusion from the perspective of students in CBLT concerning whether the teacher's focus is on content or language, teachers need to be very aware of their own use of language and how they interact with students. They need to ensure that oral communication is clear and that it serves the dual purpose of supporting both content and language learning. In this respect, prompts may be more effective than recasts in CBLT. Unlike recasts, prompts cannot be perceived by the student as a mere confirmation of the message or as another way of saying the same thing. Moreover, prompts are not accompanied by signs of approval, which often accompany recasts. Signs of approval include affirmations such as *yes*, *that's right*, and *OK*, as well as praise markers such as *very good*, *bravo*, and *excellent*. The use of such signs of approval is typical of CBLT, where teachers and students alike are more focused on content than on language. In CBLT, signs of approval serve to say "yes" to content while recasts are supposed to say "no" to form, with the inevitable result that some learners are more likely to notice the approval of content than the grammatical modification in a recast.

Reflection

If you were teaching content through your students' L2, can you think of ways that would allow you to approve the veracity or meaning of their nonnative-like utterances without letting them think the form was correct?

There is some evidence that students in CBLT contexts benefit more from prompts than from recasts, and the benefits are attributed to the depth of processing that results from pushing learners to self-repair. Recasts are considered less effective in cases where they could be perceived ambiguously as approving their use of nontarget forms or where learners have reached a developmental plateau in their use of the nontarget forms. That is, continued recasting of what students already know is not an effective strategy for ensuring continued L2 development. At the same time, continued prompting of learners to draw on what they have not yet acquired is equally ineffective. Accordingly, there is a growing consensus that students are most likely to benefit from a variety of CF types than from only one type at the expense of others.

For teachers to effectively provide a variety of CF types, they need to make choices in accordance with linguistic targets, interactional contexts, students' age and proficiency, and the classroom's communicative orientation and curricular objectives. For example, based on recent research findings, recasts may be well suited for pronunciation errors, whereas prompts may be more effective for errors in morphosyntactic features of which students already have some knowledge (e.g., subject-verb agreement). Younger learners might benefit more from prompts than recasts, whereas older learners may benefit equally from both prompts and recasts. When the error has to do with a binary choice such as grammatical gender or *be/have* distinctions, prompts are likely more effective than recasts. Finally, if the class is already language oriented, recasting may be sufficient; if the class is very much focused on content, then prompts will do a better job of bringing language to the forefront.

Quiz

Take the following quiz to see what you have learned so far. Answers are given at the end, so try not to look ahead until you are finished.

1. Which of the following programs must offer at least 50% of the curriculum in the target language to be qualified as such?

    a. CLIL
    b. Submersion
    c. Sheltered instruction
    d. Immersion
    e. CBLT

2. Which programs do not aim for additive bilingualism?

    a. One-way immersion
    b. CLIL
    c. Two-way immersion
    d. Submersion
    e. EMI

3. For input to be useful for both acquisition and CBLT, it should be . . .

    a. Unenhanced
    b. Comprehensible
    c. Aural and not written
    d. Student generated
    e. None of the above

4. Which of the following statements do not accurately describe the benefits of CBLT?

    a. CBLT helps students develop strong comprehension skills
    b. Students find that CBLT is a motivating way to learn an additional language
    c. CBLT is an effective way for students to develop high levels of grammatical accuracy

    d.   CBLT can be implemented in ways that develop students' curiosity and critical thinking skills.

    e.   None of the above

5. Which of the following scaffolding techniques should teachers avoid in CBLT?

    a.   Wait time

    b.   Linguistic redundancy

    c.   Paralinguistic elements

    d.   Multimedia resources

    e.   None of the above

6. Which type of feedback has been most frequently observed in CBLT?

    a.   Prompts

    b.   Recasts

    c.   Explicit correction

    d.   Signs of approval

    e.   None of the above

    [Answers: 1.d; 2.d; 3.b; 4.c; 5.e; 6.b]

Proactive Counterbalanced Instruction

The preceding section concerned a reactive approach to CBLT that helps students to attend to language during interaction without losing sight of the content. This section describes a proactive approach to integrating language and content. A proactive approach entails an instructional sequence comprising four interrelated phases: a noticing phase, an awareness phase, a guided practice phase, and an autonomous practice phase. Each phase includes at least one activity or task. Several examples of this instructional sequence will be provided later. For now, let's define each of these phases.

The **noticing** phase establishes a meaningful context related to content, usually by means of a written or oral text in which target features have been contrived to appear more salient or more frequent. The **awareness** phase then encourages students to reflect on and manipulate the target forms in a way that helps them to become more aware of patterns that were highlighted at the noticing phase. Also known in the literature as consciousness-raising tasks, awareness activities require some degree of analysis or reflection by means of rule-discovery tasks, metalinguistic exercises, and opportunities for pattern detection.

The subject-matter or thematic content is in the foreground during the noticing phase but fades into the background during the awareness phase as students zoom in on language. It is important to separate noticing and awareness activities, despite the difficulty of doing so, to avoid focusing immediately on language without first having established a meaningful content-related context for the language focus.

The **guided practice** phase provides opportunities for students to use the grammatical features in a meaningful yet controlled context and to receive corrective feedback in order to develop automaticity and accuracy. The sequence comes full circle at the **autonomous practice** phase by returning to the content area that served as the starting point. Autonomous practice requires the use of the target-language features but in a discipline-specific or thematic context. There are fewer constraints, allowing students to use the features in more open-ended ways to develop fluency, motivation, and confidence.

As illustrated in Figure 2, the instructional sequence begins with a primary focus on content during the noticing phase then zooms in on language during the awareness phase and guided practice phase. Finally, during the autonomous practice phase, the primary instructional focus is once again on the content that served as the starting point.

To illustrate the implementation of this instructional sequence in CBLT, an example is provided from a 5th-grade French immersion classroom with students 10–11 years old. Form-focused instructional activities targeting grammatical gender in French were embedded in the children's regular curriculum materials, which integrated language arts, history, and science. A student workbook was designed to include modified versions of texts found in the regular curriculum materials, using typographical enhancement (e.g., bolding, underlining, capital letters) to highlight noun endings that reliably predict grammatical gender in French.

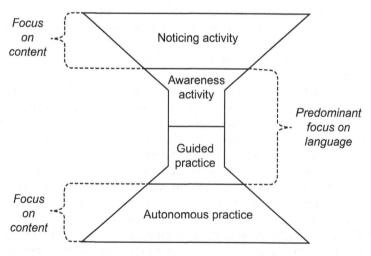

Figure 2 Instructional Sequence Integrating Language and Content in CBLT
Source: Adapted from Lyster (2016), p. 58.

The noticing activities drew students' attention to noun endings as predictors of grammatical gender. For example, in the context of learning about the founding of Quebec City in 17th-century New France, endings of target nouns and their determiners were highlighted in bold. Target words and related patterns were key to the content of the lessons. For example, *la fourrure* ("fur") was a key noun phrase because of the pivotal role of the fur trade in New France, and so was the noun phrase *la nourriture* ("food") because of the lack of food in the colony, which led to a serious outbreak of scurvy.

The ensuing awareness activities required students to detect the patterns by classifying the target nouns according to their endings and indicating whether nouns with these endings were masculine or feminine. In the case of *la fourrure* and *la nourriture*, students were expected to identify them both as feminine nouns because of their common ending—*ure*.

Then, for guided practice in attributing the right gender marker to target nouns, a set of riddles was used to review the challenges experienced by White settlers in New France and to elicit target nouns from students. For example, the riddle (provided in French) "*I am what covers certain mammals and can be made into warm coats*" was intended to elicit the noun phrase *la fourrure*. However, a student needed to say the right gender-specific determiner, which is no small feat for learners of French. Grammatical gender markers, despite their frequency, are notoriously difficult.

Finally, for autonomous practice, teachers returned to an emphasis on content objectives. They asked students to reflect on some of the differences between life in the 17th century and life today, especially with respect to social realities and values. For example, students were asked to compare the attitudes of people in New France with those of people today concerning the fashionability of fur. Even though the subject-matter goal was to have students question and compare different social realities, teachers maintained a secondary focus on language by ensuring correct use of gender, at least with key topic words such as *la fourrure*.

Keep in mind that the students were exposed to much more than the examples briefly described here, which represent only a few of the many activities that took place during the five-week instructional unit. It is important to stress that activities such as these, to be effective, entail a certain amount of repetitiveness, and so the descriptions provided here do not give the whole picture.

Three other examples follow to further illustrate the integration of language and content. These examples show the instructional sequence that makes up noticing and awareness activities followed by opportunities for both guided and autonomous practice. The first two examples integrate a focus on verb tenses into history lessons. The third example integrates a focus on grammatical gender into an environmental science class on greenhouse gas emissions. It is important to reiterate that these target-language features are difficult for L2 learners. Thus, the examples provided here are of course not sufficient on their own and need to be part of a recursive instructional approach to CBLT.

Example 1: The Passé Composé and Jacques Cartier

The *passé composé* has two parts: an auxiliary and a past participle. The auxiliary derives either from the verb *avoir* ("to have") or the verb *être* ("to be") and functions in tandem with the past participle to complete a compound verb phrase such as "*Je suis tombé*" ("I fell") or "*J'ai mangé*" ("I ate"). For the most part, auxiliary forms derive from the verb *avoir*, but a small set of high-frequency verbs use *être*. Understandably, L2 learners of French overgeneralize the use of *avoir* as an auxiliary, resulting in frequent errors such as *j'ai allé* for "I went."

What follows is an instructional sequence designed by a group of 4th-grade teachers to integrate a focus on the *passé composé* in French with their history unit on Jacques Cartier and his three voyages to the New World.

Content Objectives

- Students develop an understanding of the causes and effects of Jacques Cartier's three exploratory voyages to the New World.
- Students become familiar with the sequence of events that made Jacques Cartier a key figure in the history of Quebec.

Language Objectives

- Students consolidate their knowledge of the *passé composé* as a means to refer to completed actions in the past.
- Students hone their skills to accurately choose either *avoir* or *être* as the auxiliary verb when using the *passé composé*.

During the noticing phase, students watch a video about the life of Jacques Cartier called "La course vers le nouveau monde" ("The Race to the New World") which was prepared by one of the teachers and is available on YouTube at www.youtube.com/watch?v=_vsqzjD_oe8&feature=youtu.be. The narrative is filled with many instances of the *passé composé* using both *être* and *avoir* as auxiliaries. After watching the video, the content focus stays in the foreground as students discuss the main points surrounding Jacques Cartier's three voyages. Students take note of the dates of his travels and their effects on the subsequent influx of White settlers to what came to be known as New France.

During the awareness phase, the text of the video's narration is projected on the interactive whiteboard, with instances of the *passé composé* in bold. The teacher leads students to first identify the verbs in the *passé composé* and then together to create a list of verbs that use the auxiliary *avoir* (e.g., *grandir, donner, rencontrer*) and those that use the auxiliary *être* (e.g., *naître, partir, arriver*). An extract of the text concerning the explorer's first and second voyages is provided as an example.

Premier Voyage de Jacques Cartier

Jacques Cartier **est né** en France à St-Malo en 1491. Il **a grandi** dans une famille de pêcheurs de morue. Donc, il **a appris** très jeune à naviguer sur un bateau. En 1532, le roi François 1er l'**a choisi** pour explorer le Nouveau-Monde. En avril 1534, Jacques Cartier **a levé** l'ancre et il **est parti** avec deux navires.

Cartier **est arrivé** dans la baie des Chaleurs et **a rencontré** des Micmac (des Amérindiens) pour la première fois. Les Français **ont donné** des petits couteaux et des miroirs et, en retour, les Micmacs leur **ont donné** les fourrures qu'ils portaient. En juillet, Cartier **est arrivé** à Gaspé. Il y **a planté** une croix et il **a déclaré** que les terres appartenaient au roi de la France.

Deuxième Voyage de Jacques Cartier

En 1535, le roi François 1er **a demandé** à Cartier de partir pour une deuxième expédition. Cette fois, Cartier devait aller plus loin pour chercher un passage vers l'Asie. Il **a levé** l'ancre et il **est parti** avec trois navires.

En octobre, Cartier **est arrivé** à Hochelaga. Il y **a rencontré** des Algonquiens. Cartier **est resté** à Hochelaga une journée et il **a fait** du troc avec les Algonquiens. Il **est** ensuite **reparti** vers le royaume du *Kanata* (la région de Stadacone).

L'hiver **est arrivé** vite et **a surpris** les Français. Le fleuve était gelé et les navires ne **pouvaient** plus bouger. De plus, les Européens souffraient du *scorbut*. Cartier **a demandé** de l'aide aux Micmacs et ils **ont partagé** leur secret. Ils faisaient une potion avec des aiguilles et des écorces de pin. Jacques Cartier **a** donc **pu** sauver la vie de quelques hommes. Au mois d'avril, Cartier **est reparti** en France avec Donnacona, ses deux fils et sept autres Iroquoiens.

Troisième et Dernier Voyage de Jacques Cartier . . .

During the guided practice phase, each student receives one of five images illustrating an important event or place related to Jacques Cartier. The teacher writes on the board a list of verbs in the infinitive to be used to describe one of the events. Each student selects at least one verb from the list and writes a description of the event using the verb in the *passé composé*. Then students mingle with other students to find those with the same image, and together as a group they synthesize their descriptions to create an historical account based on the image, which they then convey orally to the whole class, giving the teacher an opportunity to provide corrective feedback as necessary.

For autonomous practice, students draw on both the linguistic and the content knowledge they gained in the preceding activities to produce, in small groups, a time line depicting some of the landmark events that punctuated Jacques Cartier's career. They illustrate the time line with the images already used and/or drawings of their own and include a legend for each key event on the time line using the *passé composé* to portray a trajectory of Jacques Cartier's experiences as an explorer. The following example illustrates how this task creates obligatory contexts for having to choose between *avoir* and *être* as the correct auxiliaries:

> *Il est né en 1491* → *En 1534, il est parti vers le Nouveau-Monde* → *Là il a rencontré les Amérindiens* → *Lors de son 2e voyage en 1535, il est arrivé à Hochelaga* → *En 1541, il a construit un fort mais n'a pas trouvé d'or* → *Il est mort en 1557.*
>
> ("He was born in 1491 → In 1534, he left for the New World → There he met Amerindians. → During his second voyage in 1535, he arrived at Hochelaga → In 1541, he built a fort but did not find gold → He died in 1557.")

As the groups present their time lines, the teacher has the opportunity to provide feedback on both language and content

Example 2: The Imperfect and the First Streetcars in Montreal

Unlike the *passé composé* and its reference to completed actions in the past, the imperfect refers to incomplete actions or ongoing states and events in the past; it thus often serves a descriptive function. The following instructional sequence was designed by a 6th-grade teacher to emphasize the uses of the imperfect for describing the first streetcars in Montreal to her social studies class. The sequence has both content and language objectives.

Content Objectives

- Students become aware of the first streetcars in Montreal and understand their evolution from horse-drawn to electric streetcars.
- Students identify the causes and effects of change specific to transportation in urban centers.

Language Objectives

- Students become aware of the function(s) of the French imperfect.
- Students use the French imperfect to describe the first streetcars in Montreal and the circumstances surrounding their implementation.

During the noticing phase, students are given images of eight different streetcars and then work in small groups to classify them from oldest to newest, explaining their choices. Then, as a whole class, they read a text about the first streetcars in Montreal in which the verbs in the imperfect are highlighted in bold. Students are asked to summarize and discuss the main points of the text (e.g., horses were injured by the salt used to melt snow during winter; the city was reluctant to bring in electric streetcars because this meant returning so many horses to pasture). The following is an excerpt from the text the students read.

Les Premiers Tramways de Montréal

À Montréal, vers les années 1860, les premiers tramways **étaient** des hippomobiles, c'est-à-dire des voitures tirées par des chevaux le long de rails installés sur la voie publique. Ce moyen de locomotion **était** assez dispendieux. C'est le chauffeur lui-même qui **faisait** la ronde pour collecter les frais de passage. Les tramways tirés par des chevaux **causaient** cependant plusieurs problèmes:

- Les wagons remplis de passagers **étaient** de plus en plus lourds à tirer par les chevaux, particulièrement dans les côtes.
- En hiver, les chevaux **subissaient** des blessures aux pattes à cause du sel répandu dans les rues.
- Le nombre de passagers **était** en progression constante.
- Le nettoyage des rues **était** aussi un problème car on **devait** ramasser les excréments des chevaux.

Les premiers tramways électriques ont fait leur apparition en Europe au début des années 1880. À Montréal, on **hésitait** à implanter les tramways électriques car cela **faisait** beaucoup de chevaux à retourner aux pâturages.

During the awareness phase, students are asked as a whole class to pinpoint the words highlighted in bold in the text, describe their forms, and discuss their meanings. In small groups, students classify the imperfect verb forms in the text as either singular or plural. Then, for guided practice, students work in groups of three to produce a short narrative describing one of the eight streetcars using the imperfect forms of at least three different verbs. For example, one group's narrative was: *Ce tramway circulait à Montréal. Il roulait sur des rails de fer et comptait environ 40 à 46 places* ("This streetcar operated in Montreal. It ran on iron rails and had about 40 to 46 seats"). They present their descriptions orally to the class, thus giving the teacher an opportunity to provide corrective feedback on the use of the imperfect. Finally, for autonomous practice, students work in small groups to conduct a research project on one of the streetcars. By means of an illustrated and annotated poster it creates, each group presents its street-car to the rest of the class in the form of historical accounts that together convey the evolution of streetcars from horse-drawn to electric. Because they must describe their streetcars and the particularities surrounding the services they provided in Montreal at the end of the 19th and the beginning of the 20th centuries, students need to use the imperfect to do so, again providing opportunities for the teacher to provide corrective feedback.

Example 3: Grammatical Gender and Greenhouse Gas Emissions

Names of countries in French must be preceded by an appropriate gender-specific determiner (e.g., *le Canada, la France*). Names of countries end-ing in "e" are feminine, with the exception of five countries: *le Belize, le Cambodge, le Mexique, le Mozambique,* and *le Zimbabwe*. All other names of countries are masculine (e.g., *le Portugal, le Canada, le Japon, le Sénégal*). In spite of these relatively simple rules, students in contexts of CBLT such as French immersion have difficulty using determiners to accurately assign gender to the names of countries.

A focus on the accurate use of determiners preceding names of coun-tries can easily be integrated into subjects such as geography or science. The following instructional sequence demonstrates how 8th-grade sci-ence students are engaged with environmental issues while drawing their attention to various countries' greenhouse gas emissions. It has both con-tent and language objectives:

Content Objective

- Students reflect on Canada's position concerning greenhouse gas emissions relative to those of other countries and on its withdrawal from the Kyoto Accord.

Language Objective

- Students identify specific countries using correct determiners.

During the noticing phase, students examine the data presented in Table 1 in order to identify and discuss the differences between the per-centage of total greenhouse gas emissions of a given country and its emis-sions per capita. At the same time, the teacher uses intonational stress to emphasize the various determiners preceding country names (e.g., *la Russie, le Brésil*).

During the awareness phase, the students are encouraged by the teacher, supported by his or her guidance as needed, to discover the rules

Table 1 Émissions de gaz à effet de serre en 2000 et pourcentage des émissions
de CO$_2$ entre 1850 et 2000*

	Millions de tonnes d'équivalent en carbone en 2000	Pourcentage du total mondial en 2000	Tonnes de carbone par habitant en 2000	Pourcentage des émissions totales entre 1850 et 2000
Les États-Unis	1892	20,7	6,6	29,8
La Chine	1356	14,8	1,1	7,3
La Russie	1283	14,0	2,8	27,2
L'Inde	506	5,5	0,5	2,0
Le Japon	364	4,0	2,9	4,1
L'Allemagne	265	2,9	3,2	7,5
Le Brésil	230	2,5	1,3	1,0
Le Canada	195	2,1	6,3	2,1
La Grande-Bretagne et l'Irlande du Nord	181	2,0	3,1	6,5
La France	137	1,5	2,3	3,0

* Adapted from Tsayem Demaze, M. (2009), Le protocole de Kyoto, le clivage Nord-Sud
et le défi du développement durable, *L'Espace géographique*, 38(2), 139–156.

that govern the grammatical gender of the names of the countries in question. Then, for guided practice, either the teacher or a student conducts a question-and-answer session, asking questions such as the following to engage students in comparing and contrasting the data in the table: *Quel est le seul pays développé qui n'a pas réduit le pourcentage de ses émissions en 2000? Quels sont les deux pays produisant le plus de gaz à effet de serre par habitant?* ("What is the only developed country that did not reduce the percentage of its greenhouse gas emissions in 2000? What two countries produce the most greenhouse gas per capita?"). Students' answers provide good opportunities for the teacher not only to provide feedback on their interpretation of the data but also to ensure their correct use of grammatical gender. Finally, the autonomous practice phase involves either an oral debate or a written argumentative essay, based on the following question: *Where does Canada stand at the international level in regard to its efforts to reduce greenhouse gas emissions and what do you think about its position?* To take a stand, students are invited to adopt a comparative approach and encouraged to accurately use determiners when referring to countries indicated in the comparisons.

A set of seven quasi-experimental studies undertaken in French immersion classrooms between 1989 and 2013 yielded overall positive effects for the integration of noticing, awareness, and practice activities on a range of challenging target features in French. In more than 75% of the 40 tests given as either immediate or delayed posttests, students participating in the form-focused tasks improved more in their use of the target forms—in both written and oral production—than students left to their own devices to "pick up" the target forms from the regular curriculum.

Teacher Collaboration and Languages Across the Curriculum

One way for teachers in CBLT to focus more on language in some contexts than others is to distribute the activities across language arts lessons and subject-matter lessons. Whereas the focus on language in the awareness phase and the guided practice phase might be best suited to language arts lessons, the greater focus on subject matter during the noticing phase and the autonomous practice might be best suited to content areas. This is fairly easy for teachers to do if they teach both language and subject matter classes. If they share these responsibilities with other teachers, this is where teacher collaboration plays a key role in CBLT.

Collaboration often occurs in schools among teachers who teach the same subject (e.g., to plan the science curriculum across grade levels) but not necessarily among teachers of the same group of students. Effective teacher collaboration in CBLT needs to occur between teachers at the same grade level who teach the same group of students, including language and content teachers. The purpose is to create coherence across the curriculum and to foster **language across the curriculum** in ways that facilitate content and language integration.

Language across the curriculum is a curricular approach, identified as such in the UK in the 1970s, which emphasizes language development across all content areas of the curriculum. Specifically, language across the curriculum makes a student's language education at school the responsibility of all teachers, regardless of their particular subject area. The main tenets of language across the curriculum are the following:

- Language develops mainly through its purposeful use.
- Learning occurs through talking and writing.
- Language use contributes to cognitive development.

Because of its emphasis on "using language to learn" and its aim to coordinate both cognitive and language development through content instruction, CBLT lends itself well to such an approach. Moreover, because many contexts of CBLT (e.g., one-way and two-way immersion programs) aim for **biliteracy**—reading and writing in more than one language—support for both target languages needs to be provided across the curriculum in ways that strengthen cross-linguistic connections.

Teachers can plan, for example, in collaboration with a partner teacher who teaches the other language to the same group of students, to read the same storybooks in both languages, alternating the reading of one chapter in one language and another chapter in the other language. Prior to each read-aloud session, teachers can ask their students to summarize the content of the previous reading, which would have taken place in the other language of instruction, and after each reading they can ask their students to make predictions about the next chapter, which will again be read in a different language. Bilingual read-aloud projects that have been conducted in this way have revealed a great deal of enthusiasm on the part of students, who demonstrated detective-like skills as they discovered linguistic similarities and differences between the two languages. Making cross-linguistic connections through teacher collaboration helps to create coherence across the curriculum. It has also been shown to increase students' engagement with the content, as they perceive the involvement of two teachers rather than only one.

There is also considerable potential for cross-curricular integration in CBLT, as illustrated in Figure 3. In addition to showing connections across languages, this model illustrates connections between content areas, specifically between science and social studies as two popular examples of content areas in CBLT, but there are of course others. In this model, teacher collaboration promotes integrated learning across target languages while also making coherent connections across content areas. What holds together the various components of the integrated curriculum is the scaffolding that all teachers need to provide to support all learners.

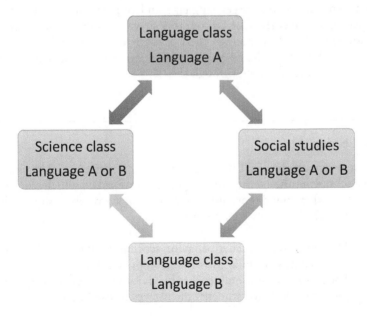

Figure 3 Cross-Curricular and Cross-Linguistic Connections in CBLT

Source: Adapted from Lyster (2016).

Elementary school teachers are already well positioned to adopt such an integrated approach. Examples from this module on CBLT include a focus on grammatical gender during the study of countries' greenhouse gas emissions, on the *passé composé* during the study of Jacques Cartier, and on the functions and forms of the imperfect during the study of the first streetcars in Montreal.

In the upper-grade levels of a French immersion program, an example might involve making thematic connections between novels studied in French and English language arts, such as Victor Hugo's *Les Misérables* and Charles Dickens's *A Tale of Two Cities*, given that they were published at almost the same time. In the social studies class, one might study the French revolution or examine the effects of 19th-century industrialization on social conditions. In science, one might study the molecular forces at play behind the steam power that gave rise to the proliferation of factories during the industrial revolution.

L1-L2 Connections in CBLT

Planning for connections between language classes to create coherence across the curriculum does not mean using the students' L1 to help them understand the content. To facilitate comprehension of a language students are still learning, teachers can use the various scaffolding techniques identified earlier. The purpose of CBLT is to create an environment in which exposure to the target language and opportunities to use it are optimal. Consequently, CBLT programs strive to circumvent the use of the students' L1. Nonetheless, there is a growing research interest in examining the role of the L1 as a cognitive tool for L2 learning and also for subject-matter learning through the L2.

Reflection

In a recent study of CLIL programs in junior vocational secondary schools in the Netherlands, students were asked which teacher behavior they found most useful to help them learn subjects through English L2. The study found that:

- The most useful teacher behavior, scoring far above all the others, was the continual use of English by teachers.
- The second most useful teacher behavior was teachers' ongoing encouragement for students themselves to use English.

In light of these findings, can you think of any good reasons to use the students' L1 in CBLT?

Context is a determining factor in making decisions about L1 use in CBLT. On one hand, minority-language students in contexts of CBLT such as sheltered instruction or transitional programs for English language learners (ELLs) in the United States are certain to benefit from use of their L1 to help them make sense of the content. There is considerable evidence that ELLs benefit from maintaining their L1 and using it as a resource for learning English and subject matter taught in English. In fact, L1 support in this way usually helps to consolidate their English language skills. If their L1 is not part of the school curriculum, ELLs need to be encouraged to draw on their home language not only to help them to engage with complex subject matter but also to validate the multifarious functions of their home language.

On the other hand, majority-language students whose L1 is English are unlikely to benefit as much from use of their L1 given its high status in an English-dominant society that tends to militate against use of non-English languages. Even in contexts of Spanish-English two-way immersion programs, students often switch from Spanish in order to accommodate L1 speakers of English. In contexts where English L1 students are learning a minority language, sustained use of the non-English language is more beneficial for pushing its development (given sufficient scaffolding to sustain its use) than recourse to English, because retrieval of target-language representations and their subsequent production are known to strengthen associations in memory in a way that makes them easier to access during spontaneous production. Providing majority-language students in this way with the support they need to "think in the immersion language" rather than "think about the immersion language through English" is likely to lead to higher levels of fluency over time. Research has already reported extensive use of English by students in Spanish or French immersion programs, increasingly so as they progress through the program. However, there is as yet no convincing evidence that English L1 students benefit from use of their L1 in moving their L2 proficiency forward. The pressing issue, therefore, is to identify the scaffolding techniques that teachers can use without the L1 to enable students to engage with increasingly complex content in the immersion language.

Putting into question the effectiveness of L1 support in CBLT raises the perennial question of translation, which needs to be qualified in terms of who is translating: the teacher or the students. On one hand, teachers in CBLT are advised not to rely extensively on concurrent translation to facilitate comprehension because immediate provision of translation equivalents reduces the students' depth of processing, thus diminishing the extent to which the target word is engraved in memory. Students are more likely to remember a word in the L2 if they have been pushed to think about its meaning through the L2 than if they are simply told the L1 equivalent in English at the outset. Moreover, the use of translation equivalents in CBLT tends to reorient the instructional focus away from contextualized academic content learning and more toward the learning of decontextualized vocabulary items. To avoid translating, teachers can draw on the scaffolding techniques outlined previously, strategically using redundancy and paralinguistic clues to facilitate understanding.

Students, on the other hand, can hardly avoid searching for translation equivalents as they process content through their L2. Making connections across languages in this way has the potential to increase depth of processing and thus to foster consolidation of content knowledge. In a recent study of German-speaking CLIL students individually solving math problems in English, it was shown that CLIL students engaged in longer phases of text comprehension than did monolingual speakers of German solving the same problems in German because the CLIL students often resorted to their L1 to test provisional interpretations of the problems. Drawing on two languages rather than only one extended their engagement with mathematical content. This engagement provided additional opportunities for switching their attention recursively between language and content. As a result, switching between languages contributed to a more profound use of the text for deducing a mathematical model to solve the problems. This is a good example of students using their L1 as a cognitive tool not just for ascertaining translation equivalents but also for processing the content. Their use of two languages apparently enhanced their engagement with the content.

Even though concurrent translation is not recommended as an instructional strategy in CBLT, making explicit connections between students' L1 and L2 is highly recommended for supporting the development of biliteracy in CBLT programs. Keeping the target languages completely separate, without making cross-linguistic comparisons, is no longer considered an efficient way to foster biliteracy development. In a planned and systematic way, teachers are encouraged to guide students in detecting similarities and differences between the two target languages. They can do so through **cross-linguistic awareness activities** that may involve cognate instruction or the study of word families and patterns in derivational morphology. In this way, L1-L2 connections are made not in the form of concurrent translation to facilitate comprehension but rather at a metalinguistic level to enhance students' cross-linguistic awareness and their ability to detect similarities and differences in patterns across languages. The purpose is to foster bidirectional transfer from L1 to L2 and from L2 to L1 in ways that contribute to reading and writing skills in both languages.

Teachers can also nurture cross-linguistic awareness by engaging in the bilingual read-aloud projects mentioned in the previous section. Partner teachers can co-design and implement biliteracy tasks related to the shared storybooks that begin in one language during its allotted class time and continue in the other language during its class time. In this way, each target language remains the language of communication in its respective classroom. This is important, because competition between target languages for time and status in school settings often leads to the habitual use of one language over the other, so the notion of each language having its own space remains crucial.

Reflection

Read the following extract from a 3rd-grade French immersion classroom and decide how you would respond to the student's reference in English to "fog." What would be more effective: acknowledging that *brouillard* is indeed the translation equivalent of "fog" or to let students try to describe fog using their L2? How accurate are their descriptions of fog? How would you describe fog in your L2?

T: *Qu'est-ce que ça veut dire, le brouillard? Tu as une idée, Justin?*
     [What does *brouillard* mean? Do you have any idea, Justin?]

S1: *C'est comme, je sais pas comment dire en français. C'est fog.*
     [It's like, I don't know how to say it in French. It's *fog*.]

T: *Je suis pas bonne avec mon anglais. Est-ce que c'est la bonne traduction? On va aller avec un mot français . . .*
     [I'm not good with my English. Is that the right translation? Let's go with a French word.]

S2: *C'est comme, quand tu rentres dans du brouillard, c'est comme du gaz qui se promène partout.*
     [It's like, when you go into fog, it's like gas that's going all over the place.]

T: *Oh là là! Mmm. . . .*

S3: *C'est pas comme du gaz mais c'est comme de la fumée. . . .*
     [It's not like gas, but it's like smoke. . . .]

Quiz

Take the following quiz to see what you have learned in this second part of the module. Answers are given at the end, so try not to look ahead until you are finished.

1. Shifting their attention between language and content is predicted to have this effect on students:

    a. Confuse and frustrate them
    b. Increase their depth of cognitive processing
    c. Improve their translation skills
    d. Make them lose sight of the content
    e. All of the above

2. Which two of the following instructional phases require more focus on language form than the other two?

    a. Noticing activity
    b. Awareness activity
    c. Guided practice
    d. Autonomous practice
    e. Reading content

3. Of the following techniques used in CBLT, which does not foster the type of comprehensible input that supports L2 development?

    a. Gestures
    b. L1 translation
    c. Facial expressions
    d. Paraphrases in L2
    e. Synonyms in L2

4. Solving mathematical problems through an L2 in CBLT is likely to . . .

    a. Diminish the students' understanding of the math concepts
    b. Prevent students from deducing a mathematical model to solve the problem
    c. Require students to rewrite the problem in their L1
    d. Extend students engagement with the problem and their depth of processing
    e. Reduce the amount of comprehensible input they receive

5. The best way to learn to read and write in two different languages is by . . .

    a. Keeping both languages separate in order to avoid confusion and interference
    b. Developing awareness of similarities and differences across the two languages
    c. Developing literacy skills in the L1 before attempting to read and write in the L2
    d. Avoiding reliance on cognates because most cognates are false friends
    e. None of the above

6. Which of these statements about students in CBLT is false?

    a. They do not draw on metalinguistic awareness to develop high levels of academic literacy in the L2
    b. They develop strong comprehension skills and high levels of communicative ability
    c. They are motivated by the content focus and its connections to the real world

d.   They do not need to translate the content in order to understand it
e.   All of the above

[Answers: 1b; 2bc; 3b; 4d; 5b; 6a]

Summary and Conclusion

This module began by illustrating the many varieties of CBLT along a continuum from language-driven programs to content-driven programs across a range of international contexts and at all levels of education. The module then highlighted some of the common pedagogical concerns shared across such diverse contexts. Specifically, given that students can bypass much grammatical structure while still processing the content, we raised the question of how teachers can more effectively juggle both language and content in ways that move students to even higher levels of target-language proficiency. Teacher scaffolding was outlined as a primary means in CBLT to provide students with the amount of assistance they need until they are able to function independently, in terms of both comprehension and production. A counterbalanced approach to CBLT was then put forth as a means to interweave language and content both reactively and proactively for the purpose of shifting students' attention more systematically between content and language.

A reactive approach to content-and-language integration was presented as a means to support students as they engage with content through a language they are still learning. To ensure engagement with the content as well as continued language growth, teachers need to ask the right kinds of questions and be strategic in their use of corrective feedback. The goal is to ensure that oral interaction is a key source of both content and language learning in CBLT.

A proactive approach was outlined as an instructional sequence targeting both content and language objectives by means of noticing and awareness activities followed by guided practice and then autonomous practice. Several examples of the sequence were provided to illustrate the feasibility of beginning with a primary focus on content during the noticing phase, then zooming in on language during the awareness and guided practice phases before returning to a primary focus on content during autonomous practice.

Language across the curriculum was then presented as a key tenet of CBLT, and teacher collaboration was highlighted as one way to ensure its implementation. In addition to cross-curricular connections, especially in school-based programs, cross-linguistic awareness was introduced as a key to successful biliteracy development in instructional settings aiming for additive bilingualism. Students' use of their L1 in CBLT was presented mainly as having a metalinguistic function, which can feed into the kind of cross-linguistic awareness students need in order to develop high levels of biliteracy.

CBLT has much promise as it continues to expand and evolve. As it does, with its flexibility in educational levels, target languages, and academic subjects associated with each target language, CBLT has the versatility to be adapted in a range of educational settings for diverse purposes. Although not a panacea by any means, the framework presented in this module for systematically integrating language and content is intended to support teachers in content-based classrooms who wish to integrate a greater focus on language as well as teachers in language-focused classrooms who are inspired to increase their students' motivation through CBLT.

Suggested Further Readings

Berger, A. (2015). Conceptualizing the interaction between language and mathematics: An Integrated Language and Mathematics Model (ILMM) of word problem solving processes in English as a foreign language. *Journal of Immersion and Content-Based Education, 3*(2), 285–313.

Cammarata, L. (Ed.). (2016). *Content-based foreign language teaching: Curriculum and pedagogy for developing advanced thinking and literacy skills.* New York: Routledge.

Day, E., and Shapson, S. (1996). *Studies in immersion education.* Clevedon, UK: Multilingual Matters.

Denman, J., Tanner, R., and de Graaff, R. (2013). CLIL in junior vocational secondary education: Challenges and opportunities for teaching and learning. *International Journal of Bilingual Education and Bilingualism, 16*(3), 285–300.

Echevarría, J., Vogt, M., and Short, D. (2008). *Making content comprehensible for English learners: The SIOP model.* Boston, MA: Pearson Education.

Hüttner, J., Dalton-Puffer, C., and Smit, U. (2013). The power of beliefs: Lay theories and their influence on the implementation of CLIL programmes. *International Journal of Bilingual Education and Bilingualism, 16*(3), 267–284.

Lightbown, P. (2014). *Focus on content-based language teaching.* Oxford: Oxford University Press.

Lyster, R. (2007). *Learning and teaching languages through content: A counterbalanced approach.* Amsterdam: John Benjamins.

Lyster, R. (2016). *Vers une approche intégrée en immersion.* Montreal: Les Éditions CEC.

Swain, M. (1996). Integrating language and content in immersion classrooms: Research perspectives. *The Canadian Modern Language Review, 52,* 529–548.

Tedick, D., and Cammarata, L. (2012). Content and language integration in K–12 contexts: Student outcomes, teacher practices, and stakeholder perspectives. *Foreign Language Annals, 45*(S1), §28–§53.

Discussion Questions and Projects

1. Corrective feedback (CF) provided during teacher-student interaction in CBLT is considered an important way of providing useful information about language to students, especially in the absence of

explicit lessons about language. And yet, in earlier conceptualizations of CBLT, CF was thought to be incompatible with the approach, given CBLT's primary focus on content. Still today, according to research, some teachers express a reluctance to provide CF in CBLT, often claiming that their students do not want to receive any. Interestingly, however, this same research shows that students actually express a strong preference for receiving CF from their teachers and sometimes complain that their teachers do not provide enough. Discuss this paradox with your classmates, on the basis of your own experiences and beliefs. To guide your discussion, choose some of the following questions to address:

a. What types of errors do you believe are important to correct, and why?

b. Is it more important to correct written or oral errors (or equally important)? Explain.

c. Is it possible to provide corrective feedback without breaking the flow of communication?

d. Discuss the pros and cons of providing more opportunities for learners to self-repair.

e. Is it more important to provide feedback in the language arts class than in subject-matter classes? Why or why not?

f. How might a student's age and grade level influence a teacher's decision to either provide corrective feedback or not? If the teacher does provide corrective feedback, how might age and grade level affect the type of corrective feedback?

2. An observational study of French immersion classrooms in Canada and Japanese immersion classrooms in the United States was undertaken to compare patterns of corrective feedback. In both contexts, most students were White middle-class children in the 4th or 5th grades. In both contexts, teachers used similar proportions of recasts and prompts. However, the ways in which the students responded to the recasts were quite different across contexts, with students in Japanese immersion repeating most of the teachers' recasts and students in French immersion repeating only very few of the recasts.

Why do you think that students' responses to recasts were so different across these contexts? In addition to possible cultural factors that you might consider, here is a description of the teachers' backgrounds to take into account:

• *French immersion*: The teaching experience of three of the four teachers prior to immersion was in L1 (not L2) classrooms; two teachers were native speakers of French, and two were French/English bilinguals (having grown up with both languages).

- *Japanese immersion*: One teacher had taught in Japan and the other in the United States as a Japanese teacher at the high school and college levels; both were native speakers of Japanese.

3. Propose a set of two language arts activities that you could do with a partner teacher teaching the same group of students as you but in the "other" language. The activities should alternate between languages around the same theme or topic but *must not be a repetition of the same task*. First, identify a content-related topic or a storybook that you could use in both languages, then propose two interrelated activities involving the same topic or storybook:

   a. Activity 1 will begin in one language in one class.
   b. Activity 2 will continue in the other language in the other class.

4. Identify a topic in a content area or a language arts theme that you teach. Then identify a language feature related to this topic or theme that you believe L2 learners find challenging. Using the instructional sequence illustrated in this module, propose a content-based unit that integrates a focus on your selected target feature(s). The instructional sequence should include at least four interrelated activities:

   a. A noticing activity designed to make the language features more salient and/or frequent in a content-related text.
   b. An awareness activity that requires learners to manipulate or reflect on the language features in a way that engages them in some degree of analysis or inductive rule discovery.
   c. A guided practice activity that pushes students to use the features in a meaningful yet controlled context with feedback in order to develop automaticity and accuracy.
   d. An autonomous practice activity related to content that encourages students to use the features in more open-ended ways to develop fluency, motivation, and confidence.